Sprir

Springtime in the Church

by

BARRY KISSELL

HODDER AND STOUGHTON
LONDON SYDNEY AUCKLAND TORONTO

 First printed 1976. ISBN 0 340 20683 7.
 Printed in Great Britain for Hodder and Stoughton Limited, London by Cox and Wyman Ltd., London, Reading and Fakenham.

To Mary, my wife, my best friend

Acknowledgments

I wish to thank:

John and Gay Perry, whose ministry inspired this book. Margaret George, who corrected my English. Leslie Davis, who deciphered the original and typed a manuscript.

The Body of Christ at St. Andrew's.

Contents

I

It's Springtime

JONATHAN, THE VICAR's five-year-old son, stood looking at Lottie. Her neck was supported by a surgical collar, and she stooped as she smiled at him. She had come to the vicarage to babysit.

'What's the matter with you neck?' inquired Jonathan, with the openness of a five-year-old.

'It's weak and needs supporting,' replied Lottie, who had had an arthritic spine for six years, and suffered much pain from a lump the size of a fist at the back of her neck.

'Have you asked Jesus to heal you?' asked Jonathan.

Lottie struggled for a moment.

'Jesus doesn't heal everyone you know.'

'Well, if Jesus can't, do you think that Jesus and God together could?'

I was with one of our 'faith-sharing' teams in the little Suffolk town of Woodbridge. We had finished the last conference session of the day, and people were talking in groups. Lottie drew me aside to share this incident about Jonathan. She had been unable to escape the words 'Have you asked Jesus to heal you?'

Lottie had been a follower of Christ for most of her

seventy years. She had accepted the specialist's diagnosis concerning her spine, and realised that it was a condition she had to live with. She daily prayed for strength to bear the pain. Now the Holy Spirit seemed to be opening up before her the possibility of healing. As she pondered the Lord said, 'I will heal you.'

Jonathan's father had experienced God's healing power in his previous parish. His own wife had been healed. Consequently, he made it known that he would regularly pray for the sick with the laying-on-of-hands. Lottie, as an outcome of Jonathan's words, went for prayer. The lump on her neck disappeared. Three weeks later she discarded her surgical collar. Her doctor confirmed that her arthritic condition was healed.

Lottie is part of the new springtime in the church. A springtime in which the experiences of the New Testament are being repeated with Christians seeking for the New Testament reality and finding it, with individuals discovering new life as the Holy Spirit is released within them. Whole communities are being reborn and making a common life. It is happening world-wide, from South America to Asia, among many races.

Two years ago I witnessed it in New Zealand where I was born. I was in Auckland which has one of the finest harbours in the world. Pale gold sand covers the beaches and these in turn give way to green-clad hills. The city is built on a series of hills. Half-way up Symonds Street, and overlooking the harbour stands St. Paul's Anglican church. With my wife Mary and our children we went to the family eucharist. A group of musicians led the worship, in a full church, from their own arrangement. After the service we met the vicar, Archdeacon Kenneth Prebble.

We had never met before, and he did not know my name, but without hesitation he asked, 'Will you preach this evening?'

The previous week the vicar had been praying about the Sunday sermons. The Holy Spirit had told him what he was to preach in the morning, but that a visitor would arrive for the evening. He made no preparation for a second sermon, leaving this entirely with God. He saw me as the person God had supplied.

Eight years before I met Kenneth Prebble he began attending house meetings where Christians were examining the gifts and ministry of the Holy Spirit. A vivid sense of the presence of God led him to seek deeper things. A springtime began to break forth in his church, with people gathering for prayer and Bible study. Spiritual freedom and zest came into their stylised form of Anglo-Catholic worship. There were problems but the congregation doubled.

When I preached that evening to a congregation which included men in dark suits and ladies in hats, alongside young people in jeans, shorts and bare feet, I was conscious of the wonderful unity which bound them together.

From New Zealand to India. I saw the beginnings of a similar movement of the Spirit when I was invited to accompany the Rev. Michael Harper on a tour of the Church of South India. Several bishops had asked Michael to make this tour. Our ministry was mainly to presbyters, although in every city we had a public meeting, chaired by various church leaders, including bishops of the Church of South India and a Roman Catholic archbishop. At Masulipatuam we met the Rev. G. O. Poornachandra Rao, then presbyter of a Church of South India at Vishalchrapatuam.

Chandra, as he was known, had built up his congregation with his out-going personality. His church secretary asked whether he would organise a series of renewal meetings. As he thought about this Chandra realised his own need of renewal.

'Lord, revive me,' he prayed.

At the final renewal meeting Chandra turned to give the benediction. As he raised his arms to pray he saw Jesus standing in the doorway of his church. Their eyes met. Chandra was filled with an indescribable love and feeling of acceptance.

In his hands Jesus carried a white leather bag.

'What's in the bag, Lord?' Chandra asked. 'What have you brought for us?'

'My son,' Jesus replied, 'I have brought blessings for you and your congregation.'

By now the people had lifted their heads and were looking at their presbyter. Chandra told his people not to leave the building because Jesus was present and wanted to bless them. As he spoke many were healed and delivered from the fear of evil spirits.

Chandra fell on his knees and confessed the sins which had led him into a spiritual winter. He was in agony of spirit. As some elderly members of the congregation rose and prayed for him he began to accept the cleansing and forgiveness which Jesus offered.

In the doorway of the church where Jesus stood was a man with throat cancer. He could only breathe through a tube inserted in his throat. For three years he had been unable to sleep, receiving his only nourishment through drinking milk from a spoon. He went home from the service and slept soundly and on awakening found that his throat had been healed. He ran to Chandra's house clutching a large piece of bread and a glass of milk. Joyously, he consumed both. Together they praised the Lord.

A Hindu woman who was at the service had suffered for years from a daily discharge. It was the following day when she too realised she had been healed. She returned to the church and Chandra led her to faith in Jesus Christ. Later she was filled with the Holy Spirit. Her husband, a Hindu Brahmin, was so impressed with her changed life that he became a believer. They were both baptised, taking the forenames of Daniel and Naomi.

I preached at a Roman Catholic compound in Bandra, a suburb of Bombay. Our official programme had ended, and Michael had left for Australia and New Zealand. When I arrived with my host, Alan Vincent, the building was packed with Indian families singing praises to the Lord. A priest led the worship. The previous evening he had told me how for years he had longed to experience the reality of God. On Sunday evenings after Mass he had gone in the dark to a hall where the Pentecostals met. He had stood in the courtyard at the rear of the building and listened to the praise and worship. One evening he begged the Lord to fill him with the same Holy Spirit. His prayer was answered and his ministry transformed.

Other priests and nuns had also entered into this fullness of the Spirit. The renewal was now spreading through the congregation. Many were inviting Hindu neighbours to the services, where they were finding Christ.

From India to Canada. Merv and Merla Watson came from there on a tour of England with their production of Shekinah. Besides playing to an enthusiastic congregation in York Minster they also visited parish churches, including Chorleywood, twenty miles from London, where I am now based. The Shekinah Company consisted of sixty musicians and dancers. Their aim was to show how the prophecies relating to Christ in the Old Testament were fulfilled in Jesus. Our congregation danced and sang with them to Jewish music. That night a Jewish girl who accompanied my wife accepted Christ as her Messiah.

Nothing is dull and drab when the Holy Spirit takes charge. He hovers over chaos bringing order and form. He is the author of creativity, seeking to inspire men to create in honour of the Risen Christ. Latent gifts are released. Groups compose their own songs and music. Parishes use their individual settings to Holy Communion. Dance and drama become a part of worship. Gifts like flower arranging, art and embroidery are offered in praise of God.

In the early sixties I was a speaker at a Fountain Trust Conference in Torquay. On the Sunday morning when we celebrated Holy Communion heaven itself descended, and time was suspended. Although the leader kept to the structure of the liturgy there was spontaneous praise, worship, prayer and prophecy. Since then I have been privileged to visit many parishes where there have been similar experiences. Holy Communion, which for some evangelicals had been an optional extra at the end of Mattins, and for others a stylised ritual, has become the centre of the church's family life. Often at this service the sick are prayed for. Here, in the atmosphere of love and faith, the gifts of healing are given by the Holy Spirit.

I have experienced nature's springtime in two hemispheres. In my native New Zealand it comes as it does in England but not as such a definite season. The barrenness and apparent deadness of winter begin to awaken as an old man from sleep. There is a stretching and a turning in the creation. Little buds appear. As the days lengthen a new potential is released. Daffodils flower among the lambs which gambol, and race each other in quick sprints. Bare trees are covered with light green leaves through which the gentle sun sparkles. The farmyards become the nurseries for the chicks and ducklings, and the stalls protect the new-born calves.

Springtime is coming just as surely to the church as the Holy Spirit is allowed to release his life within the believer. As Christians are renewed they are gathering to share a common life. This is a book about God's springtime.

2

On a Rugby Pitch

WE RESTED ON A crag above a plateau. On the edge of the bush the deer grazed in the early morning. Our climb up from the Wanganui River had begun in darkness, and now light was beginning to cast its rays upon the near end of the plateau. Our clothes were wet with perspiration and our hunting rifles weighed heavily on our shoulders.

Directly below us the trees were showing the first signs of spring. Everywhere there was new growth and life. Behind us a tui bird sang and its call was answered from deep in the bush.

As we sat I looked to our right. Far below like an eel curved the river. Above the river and on the far side were a series of ranges stretching like rolling waves to the snow-capped mountain peaks of Tongariro, Nhaurhoe and Ruapehu. To our left smaller foothills eventually gave way to a horizon formed by the Tasman Sea. Dominating the skyline and appearing to rise from the sea was the cone-shaped Mount Egmont.

Gradually, in a unique and almost indescribable way, I became aware of creation. Its beauty and wonder dawned on my mind as if released by a force outside myself. I saw beyond the bush, the river, and the mountains. Suddenly my mind was filled with a single word — God.

I became conscious of eternity, of a reality outside the material, of God himself. As a dream fades on waking, so the moment began to pass, and I became conscious again of my immediate surroundings. I was nineteen. My religious upbringing had been traditional—Sunday school, church youth club and confirmation.

The day passed and again I was absorbed with my work as a trainee stock-agent auctioneer. However, I found myself reflecting more and more on my experience in the mountains. I realised that somehow God had spoken. Previously he had been like a ruler who lived in a far away place. I had believed in his existence, but this had led neither to a positive nor a negative reaction in my life-style. Belief in his existence was purely neutral. If he did not exist, I would have lived the same.

God's existence is impossible to prove, I told myself. The ultimate proof would be to see him, and nobody had ever done that to my knowledge.

I supposed creation itself must be the greatest argument for his existence. I knew that two thousand five hundred years ago a young sheep farmer, destined to be a Jewish king, recorded his thoughts concerning this:

> The heavens are telling the
>   glory of God;
> and the firmament proclaims
>   his handiwork.
> Day to day pours forth speech,
>   and night to night declares
>   knowledge.
> There is no speech, nor are there words;

their voice is not heard;
yet their voice goes out through
all the earth,
and their words to the end of
the world. (Ps. 19: 1–4.)

The creation was a silent sermon and it continued to preach to me.

Driving up the road which ran by the side of the lower reaches of the Wanganui River, I was constrained to stop and climb a steep hill at the side of the road. From the top the road was out of sight, and as I stood still, I again experienced an overwhelming sensation of the presence of God. Instinctively, I raised both hands into the air and walked around the hilltop praising the God whom I did not know. Eternity for a second time broke into the present. Again, I became absolutely sure of a reality which I could neither see nor touch, a reality which had no form, but whose invisible presence drew from the very depths of my being a response of praise and adoration. I remember wondering what my friends would have said if they had seen me with both hands in the air apparently speaking to myself.

After this second mountain experience, the question deepened, 'Who is God?' A search began. I went to various Anglican churches; but the psalm chanting, archaic language and sermons on social issues and moral behaviour did little to meet my growing need.

One day I finished work early, and walked across the old Wanganui Bridge. I stood by the road to hitch-hike to my parents' home in Marton. A man drew up in an old Ford van.

We had not been travelling long when he began to

question me regarding my religious beliefs. I felt self-conscious, and cornered. At one stage, I almost asked to be let out of the van. He talked about heaven and hell, of judgment, of eternal life, but above all of Jesus Christ.

At last our journey came to an end, and I jumped out, with a feeling of relief. 'A religious maniac,' I told myself, but my mind retained some of his words, and Jesus began to occupy my thoughts.

A young man, who worked in a general store in our town, passed the time of day with me. Ray Muller, who was later to be ordained into the Anglican ministry, was a member of St. Peter's church in the Gonville district of Wanganui. He told me how he had become a Christian. I thought that this was a presumptuous thing to say. A Christian, to my way of thinking, was someone who helped other people like the good Samaritan. He had been born in New Zealand, and New Zealand was a Christian country, what more did he need?

Ray invited me to join a party he had organised to hear a famous American preacher in Wellington. Going to Wellington was always fun, so I invited a few friends to accompany me. Dr. Billy Graham was to preach at Athletic Park, the home of New Zealand Rugby. My friends and I planned to leave the party and enjoy a pub crawl, meeting up with them again in the evening for the return journey. At the park we left the coach, but Ray insisted that I stayed with him. I was trapped.

Athletic Park is a large oval stadium. I had slept all night outside its gates at various times to see the All Blacks play the British Lions, or the Springboks or the Aussies. In fact I had almost played there myself, in a grade match between Wanganui and Wellington. For that match I was first emergency, having been replaced at first five eighth by a Maori player.

The park was full, and the proceedings had begun. It was a bit boring, and I slipped away on the pretext of going to the toilet. I hurried outside to where my friends had been. They had vanished. A car drew up in front of me. Its door opened, and out stepped Dr. Graham. He smiled as he passed. I changed my mind. I would hear what he had to say.

We arrived in the stadium simultaneously—he to preach, me to listen.

He began his sermon. There were many quotes from the Bible interspersed with illustrations. He spoke more like a man with his finger on the trigger of an automatic rifle than a Christian minister.

'If you want to know what God is like look at Jesus Christ.' His words went on into the distance. 'God is love, and that is what Jesus' life reflects. He loved the decaying leper, the blind, those racked with pain, the social outcasts, the prostitutes. From the cross he extended his love to a dying thief.'

Jesus' whole life was one of forgiveness. The fiery Peter wanted to know how many times he had to forgive. Jesus taught that there was no limit. He demonstrated that he had authority on earth to forgive men their sins. Four men brought a friend to him on a stretcher. This man was paralysed and Jesus said to him, 'My son, your sins are forgiven, rise, take up your bed and walk' (Mark 2: 1ff.).

'If you don't know God in a personal way it's because you are separated from him. The reason you are separated is because of your sin.' His voice echoed round the stadium. Separated by sin. I was separated. My sins were numerous. I wanted to receive the love and forgiveness of God. I wanted to know him.

'Jesus died upon the cross to take your sins away.' The preacher stood with his hands outstretched, illustrating the position of crucifixion. He stopped speaking; there was silence, then he repeated the words of Jesus, 'My God, My God, why have you forsaken me?' (Matt. 27: 47.) Why did God forsake his Son? Sin separates men from God, but Jesus had never sinned. He was perfect. Then whose sin was it? It was mine.

The sermon finished, and Billy Graham was praying. I acknowledged the sin in my life, and by faith asked Jesus to live within me. Gradually, I felt as if a great weight was being lifted. I was experiencing forgiveness, and finding that God loved me.

Inquirers were invited to gather on the rugby pitch. As I began to walk forward I heard the God of my mountain experience, the God and Father of the Lord Jesus Christ.

'What you have received, you are to share,' a voice whispered. My search had ended in, of all places, the Mecca of New Zealand Rugby football, Athletic Park. Here I discovered Jesus to be the Son of God. Here I received the call to share Jesus. My winter was over; a new life was being born.

3

'Thou Preparest a Table'

For a fortnight after returning from Wellington I was elated. I spent hours reading a Bible I had been given. The language was old-fashioned, but it did not matter; the words jumped out at me. Prayer became real. The folk at work knew I had become 'religious'.

I began to relate naturally to God through Jesus, and his name filled my mind. My fervour was such that I went daily to say the morning service with the vicar at seven a.m. One day when he could not make it I said the service myself. My personal life was full of joy, and I developed a concern for a number of elderly people. Then the bubble burst. It was as if I had been supported on a floating mattress until someone took the plug out.

My old faults and hang-ups returned. Had I been conned? Was it all emotionalism, as the papers maintained? Were my experiences in the mountains and in the Park flights of imagination? Could Jesus who lived nearly two thousand years ago possibly relate to me? I tried to pray and read my Bible, but the reality had gone.

I kept going over and over what had happened, remembering the places, re-living the moments. Having made such a fuss at work and in the neighbourhood about

4

A New Dimension

DURING MY LAST YEAR at the London College of Divinity in Northwood I read the Acts of the Apostles, and underlined every mention of the Holy Spirit. I saw how he came to empower the church at Pentecost and his relationship to the individual Christian. He could be lied to, and put to the test. He could be resisted, and received. He could move people from one area to another. He spoke to believers in visions and prophecy. In the early church, demons were cast out, the sick were healed, and pagans converted to faith in Christ. My mind was registering all the facts concerning the Holy Spirit and his ministry, and deep within my heart there was forming a desire for more of God. David, the psalmist, echoed my longing when he wrote:

> As a hart longs
> for flowing streams,
> so longs my soul
> for thee, O God.
> My soul thirsts for God,
> for the living God. (Ps. 42: 1–2.)

my new faith I could not back out, but how long could I maintain my position? If it was fantasy, I would eventually have to come clean. The thought horrified me.

I loved 'hitch-hiking'. There was always the adventure of not quite knowing when you would actually arrive at your destination. Combined with this was the pleasure of conversation with unknown people. I was going to visit a friend for a weekend, and was waiting at a bridge between lifts. I had packed my Bible at the top of my rucksack, and as I waited I read the first seven verses of John 14.

> Let not your hearts be troubled; believe in God, believe also in me. In my Father's house are many rooms; if it were not so, would I have told you that I go to prepare a place for you? And when I go and prepare a place for you, I will come again and will take you to myself, that where I am you may be also. And you know the way where I am going. Thomas said to him, Lord, we do not know where you are going; how can we know the way? Jesus said to him, I am the way, and the truth, and the life; no one comes to the Father, but by me. If you had known me, you would have known my Father also; henceforth you know him and have seen him.

These words began to confirm what I had originally believed. To trust God was the same as trusting Jesus, and vice versa. I dared to believe that God wanted to be my Father — one who loved, and cared and provided for every need.

I had been in a wilderness in which every truth was challenged. I had re-echoed the phrase of Thomas, 'How can we know?' I was now on the edge of the wilderness

facing out towards the fertile valley. Behind me the voice of doubt began to fade.

I was discovering that the uniqueness of Jesus was not that he had said certain things or done certain things, but that he was the Son of God. He was Jesus, the man, but he was also God the Son. Only through him could I know God as a Father.

I tried when opportunities presented themselves to share Christ, and I began to feel the call of God to leave my job at Dalgety's and become a preacher. Whenever I contemplated this, thoughts of England filled my mind, although I was a New Zealander, and loved my country.

One Saturday afternoon I was at the home of my friend Dennis Wackrow. He lay on his bed, and I sat on a chair listening to records. Nearby he had a globe of the world. I began to spin it; continents and islands flashed by. 'Dennis,' I said, 'let's hitch-hike to England.'

On Monday I handed in my notice. The manager thought I was crazy. My colleagues gave a farewell party, and I explained what I felt God was saying. Everybody listened and was kind, but I had a problem. I was saying and believing one thing, but many of my motives needed redirecting, and I had not the power to do that myself. I began to be aware that although I longed to be changed, I was unable to free myself from some fears, habits and desires.

I said goodbye to my colleagues at Dalgety's, and Dennis took a year's leave of absence from the timber company where he was employed but we nearly did not leave New Zealand. In Auckland we were joined by a few friends who had journeyed to see us off. On the morning of the embarkation I telephoned the shipping office to check the time of departure. The clerk said 6 p.m. instead

of 4 p.m. Fortunately, we all went to look over the ship at 3.55 p.m., just in time to scramble up the gangplank as it was about to be lowered.

The great ropes which held the ship to the wharf were raised. A tug guided us into the shipping lane. Our friends on the wharf became spots of colour in the distance. The throb of the engines replaced the noises of the city. 'Farewell—land of the long white cloud.' As the shores of Waitemata Harbour faded, the ship began to ride the swells of the Pacific Ocean. Standing on the upper deck, the sea breeze brought back memories of surfing and freedom. Was I being impetuous? Was the Lord really calling me to England?

Rounding Cape Farewell we left the Pacific Ocean and headed towards Australia across the Tasman Sea. The sea was a monster tossing and turning which made the sight of Sydney Harbour bridge welcome indeed. This great iron expanse heralded the eastern doorway to the Australian continent. We changed ships. Melbourne and Perth followed in quick succession, then across the Indian Ocean to the little island of Ceylon.

Often at night I climbed to the upper decks to be confronted with the power, majesty and moodiness of the sea. How this contrasted with the stillness of the universe which stretched above. At such times I knew a very real communication between my spirit and the Lord, speaking peace to my soul, reassuring me that I was on course.

We disembarked at the Egyptian port of Said. Our intention was to make our way to Jerusalem, and from there hitch-hike overland to England, which was still possible in the early sixties. It was winter when we arrived in the Holy City. My father was employed as an educational specialist with U.N.R.W.A., a branch of U.N.E.S.C.O.,

and my parents had made their home on Mount Scopus. Before leaving New Zealand, we had not thought about the weather conditions in the Northern Hemisphere, but soon realised that it would be impossible to sleep rough during the winter months We were glad of a family base.

We had three months to wait until the snows melted in the Lebanese mountains. We walked the places where Christ walked, and studied the incidents in the Scriptures. Days on end we sat in the soukes, with the Arab merchants, watching the world go by. Christmas came, and we went to Bethlehem, where the thoughts of countless millions of Christians were focused. Yet even in his land I was restless, yearning to be on the way to England.

When the weather became a little warmer we made preparations for the journey. I had walked miles in the mountains in New Zealand with a rucksack, and was conscious of how heavy it could become. I decided to take just a sleeping bag and a change of clothes.

Taking leave of my parents we walked to the old city of Jerusalem and took the road leading down to Jericho. A large diesel lorry pulled up; an Arab's head appeared through the window. I told him we were going to England. He smiled as we clambered into the cab. Little did we know that this was the first of two hundred and ten lifts in transport which included cars, trucks, motor-bikes, a horse and cart, a road grader, and a river-barge.

We journeyed on for three months, through Jordan, Syria, Southern Turkey, Greece, Austria, Germany, Holland, and finally Belgium. At night our roof was the open sky, viewed from beaches, fields and out-houses. Our bathrooms were the rivers and lakes which criss-crossed the continents. As we travelled we developed cer-

tain rules of the road. If a vehicle could only take one of us, then the one who had the first lift would wait at the boundary of the city of destination for the other. If by mischance we should be separated we would meet up at an address in England.

Every New Zealander knows about the white cliffs of Dover. They have a place in our war memories and in the minds of those who left England for a new life in Australasia. I saw them in the light of a May evening, as loneliness began to grip my heart. I looked in my wallet—just five pounds. It was all I had in the wide world.

The cross-channel ferry landed at Folkestone. I was rather conspicuous with shorts, sandals and a dilapidated pullover. The customs officer looked through my rucksack. He was a friendly sort. Once out of the customs shed I walked towards the main road, talking to the Lord, telling him of my arrival which, on reflection, he must have known about anyway.

'Lord, where am I sleeping tonight? How am I going to keep myself? Where am I going to live? What do you want me to do now I'm here?'

A car pulled up. I looked inside. It was the man in customs uniform, who had looked through my rucksack. He smiled and opened the passenger door. When I gave him an address in Hampshire, he invited me to spend the night at his house.

His car swung into the driveway of a semi-detached home on the outskirts of Dover. He called his wife, telling her there was a visitor for supper, and a guest for the night. She had already cooked a meal for three. That morning she had known there was going to be a guest that night. Being a rationalist she discarded the thought, but as

she went to town to buy supplies the impression continued, so she bought extra food and prepared it.

Coincidence? When such incidents become a regular part of life, they add up, through the eyes of faith, to something more.

I was on the road early next morning. On the outskirts of Lymington in Hampshire, I was given a lift by a farmer returning to Pennington. He asked me where I had hitch-hiked from. I told him Jerusalem and that he was the final lift to my destination, number two hundred and ten! I think he thought I was joking, but he invited me home for coffee before driving me to the home of Leslie and Phyl Davies.

Leslie and Phyl had emigrated to New Zealand, and our family had befriended them. They stayed two years. Before returning to England they gave me an open invitation to visit them. They were surprised to see me, but invited me into their home and family, an invitation which extended for two years.

I began work on a building site, as a brickey's labourer. St. Mark's, Pennington was the village church, and the vicar, the Rev. Peter Raban, gave the hand of friendship. I fell in love with a girl in the choir during the second evening service I attended. Three years later Mary became my wife.

The words from Athletic Park remained in my mind: 'What you have received, you are to share', but how was God's call to find meaning and fulfilment in England? I became homesick and longed for the mountains, the rivers, the deer, the breaking surf and the racing surfboard; for the hot sun and the sand, for the freedom to go barefoot and to lie in a field of lush New Zealand grass, to barbeque in the evenings and play Rugby football. I

became restless and wanted to be on the move again, to see new people and places.

As the months passed, the restlessness subsided, and the way opened for me to begin theological training for the Anglican ministry.

Many with whom I discussed my thoughts tried to reassure me that the Holy Spirit no longer ministered in the church today as at the beginning. The manifestations of his presence had passed away, for the church was now established. It was like telling a man in the desert without water that he no longer needed it. God had created a thirst, and I was beginning to see where the sparkling stream lay.

I came in contact with St. Andrew's, Chorleywood, a tin-roof church situated on the edge of suburbia in north-west London. John Perry was the vicar, and with his wife Gay had been invited there from Christ Church, Woking. Students at the College described it as a place which had come alive, so Mary and I went to the evening service to see for ourselves.

The church was so full we had to sit on the chancel steps. There was something going on, but I was unable to put my finger on it. Although Anglican in structure the service had tremendous life and vitality. I decided the vicar must have a strong personality!

John Perry's sermon seemed so ordinary, the exact opposite of what I had imagined. He read his text, from Acts 13: 1–4, which described the leaders of the church in Antioch, and the beginning of the first missionary journey of Barnabas and Paul. My attention had wandered, when suddenly I heard John speak the words, 'The Holy Spirit said, "I want Paul and Barnabas set apart for the work to which I have called them."' As the words sank in God said, 'You will serve me in this church.'

I could not go to an unknown vicar and tell him that, but I shared what God had said with Mary, and we prayed that if it was his will, that we would be approached by the Perrys.

John and Jenny Simons were two friends of ours who had been seconded to the parish of St. Andrew's from the College to gain pastoral experience. They invited us to attend a Friday evening prayer meeting in the vicarage. When I arrived I realised that we were on the edge of something new. I have always been sensitive to atmosphere, and was conscious of the love and interest the people had for us.

The vicarage was full, and people were sharing from the scriptures and experience. Prayer needs were made known, and concern was expressed for those in the parish in need, or suffering sickness. After a short Bible study there was prayer. At this point I realised a depth of corporate worship which I had never before known. There was praise interspersed with prayer, and intercession, and beautiful singing. I looked at my watch; it was one a.m. We had been in the vicarage four hours.

As we were leaving a rather rotund businessman asked me if I had experienced the power of the Holy Spirit. I did not quite know what he meant, but I was aware that the Spirit was the source of all that we had shared that evening.

His remark led me again to try and work out my own understanding of the person and work of the Holy Spirit.

I had a question! How could I experience the Holy Spirit in the way the New Testament taught through metaphors of fire, wind, oil and water? When I received Jesus, I had received the Holy Spirit. There could be no addition to Jesus. The scriptures say that in him 'the fullness of God was pleased to dwell' (Col. 2: 9). To receive Jesus was to receive in potential all that God wanted to share with me. It would be impossible to believe that there was Jesus plus the Holy Spirit. And yet!

Two words came to mind, 'appropriate' and 'release'. It was possible to have in potential all that God wanted to give me, but not to experience it. I needed to 'appropriate' the power of the Holy Spirit. I began to see that this would mean the 'release' of God's life which I received when I first believed.

Although Jesus nowhere used the term 'release' in respect of the Holy Spirit, he does infer such a 'release' in his conversation with the woman of Samaria.

> Whoever drinks of the water that I shall give him will never thirst; the water that I shall give him will become in him a spring of water welling up to eternal life. (John. 4: 14.)

Again he tells the crowd at Jerusalem that the Holy Spirit would flow from their hearts like fountains of living water. 'A spring' and 'a fountain' both conveying the idea of a source from which water is 'released'. How could the Holy Spirit release his life in me?

I was caught up in College work, and the fellowship at St. Andrews faded from my mind. One Friday Mary was on night duty as a nurse at Mount Vernon Hospital, Northwood, so I visited some friends. As I left our flat John Simons arrived in his car, and invited me to go with him to St. Andrew's prayer meeting. A few minutes earlier I would have missed John and an encounter which ushered in a new dimension to my Christian life.

I met Edgar Trout that night. He hailed from Plymouth, the naval city of Devon. As well as being a successful business man he was a Methodist lay preacher, and helped run the Bath Street Mission, a centre for the down and outs in the city. His ministry was transformed after experiencing a miraculous healing of his back. Because of his injury he had been confined to bed. During this time a minister visited him and commanded him in the name of Jesus to rise from his bed and walk. Astonished, Edgar spend the rest of the day running up and down the stairs of his home.

Edgar exercised the gift of the Spirit called 'the word of knowledge', (1 Cor. 12:1). An example of this gift is seen when Jesus talked to the woman at Samaria. He said:

> Go, call your husband, and come here. The woman answered him I have no husband. Jesus said to her, You are right in saying, I have no husband; for you have had five husbands, and he whom you now have is not your husband: this you said truly. (John 4: 16–17).

It is obvious from the initial conversation that they had not previously met. Similarly the Apostle Peter confronted the startled Ananias with the question, 'How can Satan have so possessed you that you should lie to the Holy Spirit and keep back part of the money?' (Acts 4: 3.)

When John and I arrived at the vicarage, Edgar was speaking on the authority which Jesus has given to the believer. Afterwards he prayed for several individuals, pinpointing their need, whether for healing of spirit, mind, body or personal relationships. He prayed for me. Nothing dramatic happened. I had taken a step of faith, believing that Jesus would 'release' his life within me.

The next morning I was in the College library revising for my final examinations. It was early, and I was alone. Looking out of the window I saw the daffodils, and the sun glistening on the dew drops. The white and pink blossom hung delicately, like a Japanese painting. The sky reflected a clear blue. I began to praise the Lord, and quite naturally and spontaneously I found myself speaking in a language I had never learnt.

Was I making the language up? I knew only English, and what I was saying was not intelligible to me. I spoke this language for some time, then began to sing in it. It seemed to me as if I was singing in sentences that somehow made sense. Jesus was very near, and my singing was directed to him. I drove to the vicarage at Chorleywood where Edgar Trout was staying. He told me that my doubts were common to those who received this gift from the Lord.

Mary was nursing at the local hospital and was on night duty. I woke her up to share what had happened that morning. She had also been praying that the Lord would fill her with his Spirit. She returned with me to Chorleywood where Edgar prayed for her with the laying-on-of-hands. John Simons was at the vicarage and as Edgar prayed for Mary, John was filled with the Spirit and began to speak in tongues. Together we were so filled with the joy of the Lord, that we sang and danced around the vicarage lounge.

Later that year a classics graduate asked me to pray with him. He knew that something was causing a turmoil in his life but could not put his finger on it. As I prayed I felt within me a deep compassion and concern for him. Not knowing how to express it I began to pray quietly for him in tongues. Afterwards, in conversation, he asked me why I had prayed for him in Latin, and not in English. He told me that while I prayed he caught the sentences, a beautiful intercessory prayer in Latin which he knew.

Three days after receiving the 'release' of the Holy Spirit I was sitting in our flat, when I had an overwhelming desire to pray for Edgar Trout. I did not know what to pray; so I prayed in the new language I had received. I felt my spirit groaning in intercession. I suddenly knew Edgar's life was in danger.

After ten minutes I telephoned to share the experience with John Perry, who in turn telephoned Edgar's home in Plymouth. He learned that a few minutes previously Edgar, on going out to his car, had been startled by a man behind him with a knife. The man tried to stab him, but was unable to do so, an invisible hand clasping his right wrist. He cried in agony as his wrist was twisted, and he was thrown to the ground. The Lord had given his angels charge over his servant.

A large proportion of Edgar Trout's ministry was spent in counselling those who were involved in Satanism and witchcraft, and wanted Christ to free them. He was a man of extraordinary faith with a deep compassion for the sufferings of his fellow men. It was this compassion which led him to give more than he was physically able. He died from a heart attack in his early fifties. Through his life and ministry I first realised there was a new springtime in the church.

My experience in praying for Edgar Trout seemed to be the Lord saying, 'Barry, you're on course; this is another landmark. Soon you will be moving into a violent storm.'

During my theological training I had learnt in small groups to share thoughts from the Bible, and to pray with others. This was known as fellowship, but it was rarely the sharing of real things. I for one didn't want to share the intimate areas of my life. I didn't want to talk too much about myself because I thought that other Christians were better, and would consider me a failure.

Although an apparent extrovert, I was shy, and suffered from long bouts of depression. For no apparent reason a cloud would begin to descend upon my mind and engulf me. During these times I could not communicate with anyone, and rejected company. I longed to be free from this burden, but the very longing often caused another bout.

I had psychological problems which went back to my childhood. Many of the problems of adulthood are a result of the hurts and conflicts experienced in the first years of life. Other painful experiences go back to the womb, and the process of birth itself. If a baby is separated from the love of its mother, then in its mind are planted fears of insecurity and rejection. In the first few months of life I was adopted. It was hard to accept this, think about it, or discuss it. It was a taboo subject.

When Edgar prayed that the Holy Spirit would be released in me, a lid was lifted off my sub-conscious. This lid was a defence mechanism which I used, to keep down the thoughts which were erupting. Now a conflict began to develop, a storm broke in my head, with the crashing of waves and the violence of wind. Bobbing about were the thoughts of rejection, insecurity and death. They had been released from the sea-bed, and I tried frantically to push them down, but to no avail.

Yet I was not without hope, for I sensed that the presence of Jesus was more than able to still the storm.

At last I gave up the fight of rejecting these negative thoughts, and began to face them. If anything the storm worsened, but the panic left me. In the past I was never able to come to terms with my depression, but now I saw the cause and in the Lord's strength faced it with courage.

I began to look rejection, insecurity, and the fear of death in the face. At night I had hideous dreams, with evil distorted figures. The Holy Spirit was spring-cleaning the recesses of my mind. Although the dreams were not pleasant, they led in the morning to a peaceful waking. The Holy Spirit had come like fire and burnt through the bands which had held down the lid of my sub-conscious. Now I longed for his healing, for it to seep into the cuts and hurts bringing wholeness.

After Ordination by the Bishop of Truro we began our ministry in the West Country. I still believed that the Lord was calling us to St. Andrew's, Chorleywood. We had prayed that if it was God's will John Perry would ask us—he hadn't!

For the first year in the West Country I felt as if I was recovering from a major operation. At times I experienced pain and sadness. The surgeon had cut deep. These cuts were an expression of his love. No one else could cut away the cancerous roots.

After his empowering by the Holy Spirit, Jesus outlined to the congregation in Caperneum his ministry. Quoting from the prophecy of Isaiah he claimed that it had found its fulfilment in himself:

> The Spirit of the Lord God
> is upon me,
> because the Lord has anointed
> me
> to bring good tidings to the
> afflicted;
> he has sent me to bind up the
> brokenhearted,

to proclaim liberty to the captives,
and the opening of the prison
to those who are bound. (Isa. 61: 1.)

Jesus can 'bind up hearts that are broken'. The heart of man is the seat of his reason and will, as well as his emotions. The psychiatrist and psychologist through their insights can find the causes of our problems, and the medical practitioners can prescribe anti-depressant drugs. Such treatment gives relief, but there is a healing of the heart, and of the deep recesses of the mind, and of the spirit, which is the prerogative of God. Besides the psychological causes there are also the satanic. I was asked to counsel a young man with an abnormal fear. He played a guitar for a band engaged on a tour of Western Germany. During this time he became interested in the occult, and took part in a number of seances. On one occasion he was asking the spirits for a message, when he felt a power going through his body. From that moment he was captive to an irrational fear, which threatened to destroy him. Prayer in the name of the Lord Jesus Christ can liberate and free from demonic powers. Healing in this area is the prerogative of the believing church. Peter in the house of Cornelius speaks of this aspect of ministry to the Roman officer, 'God has anointed Jesus with the Holy Spirit, and with power, and because God was with him, Jesus went about doing good, and healing all who had fallen into the power of the devil.' (Acts 10: 38.)

My healing from the past was gradual. At times I had lapses when I found myself in situations which would bring on again the acute fears, but the healing hand of the Holy Spirit continued to deal with me.

In our little Cornish home we had a door which had

warped and dropped. From the outside it could only be half-opened as it caught on the carpet. For a year we only ever opened the door half-way. One Saturday afternoon I decided to take it down and plane an inch off the bottom. In the evening I re-hung it. It could now swing at 90°, but we continued to open it, as we had always done, at 45°. Our minds had adopted a pattern in relationship to the door. Although the situation relating to the door had changed, our thought pattern had not. It was a number of weeks before we regularly opened the door to its full extent; even then we occasionally slipped back into our old ways.

The Lord spoke a parable to me through the door. My reactions were determined by past experiences. Now through the Holy Spirit's ministry I was free to react in new ways. He had delivered me from my bondage of fear. How appropriate the words of Paul that we are to be 'transformed by the renewal of our mind' (Rom. 12: 1).

I began to live in this new-found freedom. Gradually my reactions changed as I was confronted with fear and insecurity situations. Instead of reacting in panic, or an unwillingness to face the facts, I was able to cope—in the Lord. There were failures, and at times the old reactions overwhelmed me, but the Holy Spirit was transforming my mind.

People ask, 'Granted that we as Christians experience anxiety situations, how can we be victorious in them?' The Lord showed us the answer to this. When we went to Cornwall we lived with our family of three small children in cramped accommodation. As I was beginning a ministry, Mary was trying to cope with the problems of those who came to the door. In the end the circumstances became too much for her, and she began to suffer from anxiety. The situation worsened, and she had to remain in bed. The doctor said there was nothing organically wrong, in fact, physically she was in excellent health.

When Mary had been confined to bed for several days, leaving the children with friends, I had to go out for an afternoon. Returning after tea I went into the bedroom, and found her completely well. My first words were, 'Mary, you're better'. While I had been away, she had looked up in a concordance all the passages of scripture which referred to anxiety. In her study she had come to Paul's Letter to the Church at Philippi:

> Rejoice in the Lord always; again I will say, Rejoice. Let men know your forbearance. The Lord is at hand. Have no anxiety about anything, but in everything by prayer and supplication with thanksgiving let your requests be made known to God. And the peace of God, which passes all understanding, will keep your hearts and your minds in Christ Jesus (Phil. 4: 4–7).

Mary had taken those words literally and on the basis of them made a list of all the things which were causing her anxiety. She asked the Lord to help her, and as an act of faith thanked him. She was bathed in a wonderful peace which brought wholeness to her personality. Since that time we have called this scripture 'God's prescription for anxiety', and use it regularly, both individually and together.

5

The Power of God

JOE AND ANN had been married for four years, but because of Joe's temper the relationship could not stand the strain; they separated, and Ann took the children to live with her. She was befriended by Christians, who welcomed her into their fellowship group, and shared the good news about Jesus Christ. Gradually she came to a place of commitment, and experienced the transforming love of Jesus. Realising the change within herself she prayed for Joe.

One lunchtime Joe was at his job as a spot-welder, when he had an overwhelming feeling that he should go to a church. The last time had been at his wedding. The church that came to mind was at Chipperfield, a little village in Hertfordshire. As he drove there he began to weep, which was completely out of character.

As he sat in the quietness of the parish church, he became aware of his sin. He took a prayer book and read a section which described how Jesus died for our sin. The realisation dawned that Christ had died for him.

Nobody had told Joe about Jesus. As a child he had not been through the traditional sacraments of baptism and confirmation. He had not been taught the basics of the

Christian faith in Sunday school nor accompanied his parents to a place of worship. With Joe the Holy Spirit had taken the initiative. He had moved into his life, and communicated to him the reality of Jesus.

When Mary and I spent an evening with them, we thought they were a newly-married couple. Jesus had not only established their individual relationship with the Father, but also their relationship with each other. They had received not only the gift of a new life, but also the gift of a new marriage.

In many places there is a rediscovery of the Christian gospel. The Apostle Paul in his great treatise wrote to the Christians at Rome:

> For I am not ashamed of the gospel: it is the power of God for salvation to every one who has faith, to the Jew first and also to the Greek. For in it the righteousness of God is revealed through faith: as it is written, 'He who through faith is righteous shall live' (Rom. 1: 16–17).

This Gospel of which the Apostle writes is God's good news. It was promised centuries ago through the Hebrew prophets to the Jewish people. These prophets foresaw a time when a child would be born in the nation. He would be no ordinary child because he would be Emmanuel, which means 'God with us' (Isa. 8: 10). As this child grew to manhood he would give himself as a substitute for the sin of the people (Isa. 53: 5).

God's 'Good News' has always been about a person: about a man who was the Son of God, the Lord Jesus Christ, but he has been in danger of being lost in the shadow of the church's structure. For the church instead of being occupied with its Head and Founder has been preoccupied with its buildings and administration. I remember meeting Dick, an elderly Christian in Guildford, on the first evening of a house-party which we were conducting. At the opening meeting we asked each one to say why they had come. Dick replied, 'I've found the life and teaching of Jesus irresistible.' In the spiritual renewal which is taking place, the spotlight is again on the central figure, who was both human and divine.

Here is one who can understand our predicament, whose understanding is based upon his experience as a man. He knew hunger and thirst: he knew tragedy and joy: he knew bereavement, suffering and death. 'Jesus understands' is not a glib statement, but a fact of history.

I arrived home one afternoon to find our lounge filled with smoke. Sitting on the settee in the corner was Joyce, drinking tea and chain-smoking. After an unhappy marriage, she had that day left her husband, and was suffering from depression. She talked endlessly about her problems, apparently insurmountable. As she was leaving I said two words, 'Jesus understands'. The Holy Spirit took these words and gradually they became not just words, but truth, which in turn led to her being made whole. For Jesus can not only understand, but has infinite power to help.

The way to change society is by changing individuals. The power for this transformation is in the person of the Lord Jesus Christ. He becomes the power of God in the lives of men. People are no longer 'hopeless', and no one is beyond his reach.

I met Joanna in the kitchen of her dilapidated house. Her background was tragedy itself. Rejected by her mother, she was brought up in various children's homes.

Her journey had led her onto the streets of London, into prison, through sordid relationships, and finally to a place of hopelessness surrounded by fatherless children.

I talked to her about the transforming power of Jesus. She and a girl friend listened mockingly. I left, but the Holy Spirit remained, and a week later she burst into a room where I was taking a group meeting. In a hesitant way she said that she wanted to become a Christian, as long as she did not have to give up smoking, drinking, or men.

Jesus calls a man to come exactly as he is. Levi was a tax collector. No doubt Levi was on the fiddle and had a number of rackets at his customs post. Jesus did not confront him with the negative side of his life, but called him to come as he was. Jesus knew that once Levi came, and knew that he was accepted, a transformation would begin. Levi would then come to grips with the moral issues of his life.

This is what happened with Joanna. The Holy Spirit, through other Christians, showed her that Jesus loved and accepted her. This led to a steady transformation in her conduct and in her home.

Joanna's life is a revelation of the power of God. In every relationship God takes the initiative. This is an expression of his love and compassion. Man in no way deserves anything from God. Everything he receives is a gift. In the Scriptures forgiveness (Acts 5: 31), faith (Rom. 4: 16), eternal life (Rom. 6: 23), the Holy Spirit (Acts 2: 38, 8: 20), and Jesus Christ himself (2 Cor. 9: 15) are all referred to as the gifts of God.

A gift cannot be earned, but is an expression of love. For the Christian it is receiving the undeserved love of God. Probably the most ingrown assumption of Anglicanism is that we are working our way to heaven. The concept of grace has not been grasped.

As Joanna was discovering the grace of God, another miracle was taking place. I was preaching a series on 'Life in a New Dimension' at a polytechnic college. These were given in the new lecture hall during lunch times. I hung a large painting behind the rostrum and had it spot-lighted.

I had asked Rachel, an artist, if she would draw the back-cloth, of the crucified Christ with groups representing various strata of society passing by. While Rachel worked on this she had a dream. She was walking along a footpath when four men in a furniture van pulled up. They jumped from the van and began to pursue her with knives.

As they came closer Rachel began to cross herself in the name of the Father, Son and Holy Spirit, but still the men gave chase. In her panic she stopped and genuflected before an altar. Finally, at the point of giving up, she called 'Jesus'. She awoke, and a feeling of great peace filled her. Suddenly, she realised for the first time after over forty years of church attendance that being a Christian was trusting Jesus.

The gospel is the revelation of God's power and grace. Eight years ago a police inspector, Ivor Fox and I, organised the showing of a Christian film, *For Pete's Sake.* We hired the local school for the showing, and publicised it in the area. We were surprised when we had a full house.

The event was a total disaster. Although we had run it through prior to the performance it broke down in the first five minutes. A number of youngsters began to stamp their feet, and shout. Eventually it got under way again, and a group of girls decided to go to the toilet. They were like a herd of elephants, trumpeting as they went. Again the film broke down, and by this time I felt we should abandon the whole operation. However, Ivor encouraged me to persevere, and finally the film concluded.

As it finished I felt the Lord was saying, 'Make an invitation'. In the circumstances, I thought that this must be my own imagination, for everything had been disastrous. Ivor shared my pessimism. However, I walked to the front and, with my face as red as a lobster, invited people to stay and receive Jesus Christ into their lives. Some began to leave, others stood in groups talking. I would have given anything for the floor to have opened up and swallowed me, but it did not.

Gradually from the departing crowd a number of people walked forward and sat quietly in the front row. They all indicated that they wanted to make peace with God through faith in the Lord Jesus Christ. Their response had nothing to do with emotionalism, with atmosphere, or with personalities. The only explanation was that God's power was in our midst.

On the first evening of a house-party I met Richard. He was forty, and had a senior position in management. He had recently become interested in the Christian faith. During the weekend he attended the sessions, and on the Saturday evening he sought me out. He was sceptical of any form of Christian experience and had intellectual difficulties relating to the faith. At the end of our conversation I had to admit that I was unable to answer all his questions.

By Sunday afternoon Richard was a new man. During Holy Communion the Lord removed the veil from his mind and, in his own words, he had 'a tremendous experience of Christ'. He passed from darkness to light, from the dominion of Satan to God (Acts. 26: 18).

Christian salvation is a process which begins when a man meets Jesus Christ. His sins are forgiven, the Holy Spirit indwells him, and he receives eternal life. In another sense the follower of Christ is daily being saved. Through confession and repentance he receives the continuous forgiveness of God, through which his relationship is maintained. Our salvation will be complete when we are ushered into the presence of God.

The key to salvation is the little word 'faith'. The Scripture says, 'Without faith it is impossible to please God. For whoever would draw near to God must believe that he exists and that he rewards those who seek him' (Heb. 11: 6).

Faith is always active, never passive. It is seen when Peter steps out of the boat, on to the water, in response to the Master's call (Matt. 14: 29). It is seen as the Roman centurion returns home (Matt. 8: 10). It is seen in the woman with a haemorrhage who pushes her way through the crowd to touch Jesus for healing (Matt. 9: 20). Active faith is based upon Jesus and his words.

I was flying from Heathrow in a VC10, and prior to take-off entered with others into the nervous excitement which preludes every flight. The engines whined, and the stewardesses checked our safety belts. A steward demonstrated how life jackets are inflated. A small truck pulled us out of our bay and turned us towards the main runway.

We queued behind other aircraft. At last it was our turn. The Rolls-Royce engines screamed as the pilot released the brakes. We were thrust back into our seats as the acceleration increased. The wheels left the ground and we were off.

New laws, the laws of aero-dynamics had taken over and were governing our flight.

Faith launches us into the realm of the Holy Spirit, where the laws of God prevail. It is a dimension where the mind, intellect, and logic alone find it impossible to cope. For the ways of God are higher than the ways of man and the wisdom of God is folly to the mind of man. The cross to men without Christ is folly.

I gave a talk on salvation to the Christian Union at a northern university. The meeting had been inspired by the Holy Spirit. At the conclusion there was an open time of prayer, and spontaneously many people stood, and gave thanks and praise to the Lord.

A number of students invited me to their flat for supper. One of the girls had difficulty in walking. I had wondered about her disability. In her early teens she had had a number of lumbar punctures, which had left her partly paralysed in her legs.

After supper we sat around the fire, and she asked if we would pray for her healing. In her request she was saying, 'I have faith in the healing power of God, and would like you to pray for me.' It was obvious from our conversation that she had a high level of faith and expectancy. I read the passage from James that when such prayer is requested, those who pray are to anoint with oil in the name of the Lord. Someone produced a bottle of cooking oil. She, like a child, simply asked her heavenly Father to heal her. Together, as members of Christ's body, we laid hands on her, saying, 'Here in the name of the Lord is the answer to your prayer.'

Immediately she thanked the Lord for his healing, but when I left to travel home she was still stiff and in pain. Next morning her room-mate telephoned to tell how she had gone to bed still thanking the Lord. When she awoke all the pain had gone, and her joints were free. Previously, it had taken fifty-five minutes to walk from her hall of residence to the university. Now it took twenty!

Sometimes God heals us physically and sometimes he does not. God, however, is victorious in every situation where faith is exercised.

In a block of flats I came upon a door which was ajar. I rang, and a faint voice invited me to enter. I walked into the living room, and was called into the bedroom. Lying there, very pale, was a lady in her fifties, with a painful stomach ulcer, confined to bed. I realised that she probably tired easily, so after a brief conversation I simply read part of the Gospel narrative to her and prayed.

Next time I visited her she had deteriorated, and I soon became aware that, unknown to herself, she probably had a stomach cancer. I shared with her the healing power of Jesus. One cold winter evening I found her lying across a chair in the sitting room quietly sobbing. Between her sobs she shared her terrible fear. I prayed against this fear in Jesus' name, and laid hands upon her.

Next morning I found her sitting up in bed completely free from pain. That night she had felt as if she had been wrapped in cotton wool, suspended in a beautiful love above her bed. It was her first night free of pain in eighteen months. Jesus had become so real to her that she had become a Christian.

Later, the pain returned. She was admitted to hospital, but, although her body was decaying, a miracle was taking place as she radiated a beautiful Christlike quality of life. Before she died she showed me how Jesus meets us in our suffering.

6

Fire in the Valley

I HAVE ALREADY mentioned St. Andrew's, Chorleywood. In 1970 John Perry, the vicar, wrote inviting me to be his curate. I had never mentioned to John my earlier conviction that God was calling me to join him. I was overwhelmed by this evidence of God's guidance, and a few months later moved with my family to this lovely Hertfordshire valley.

St. Andrew's had been experiencing a springtime since John and Gay Perry came to the church in 1962. On arrival they were welcomed by a small nucleus praying for spiritual renewal. Under John's leadership they commenced a study of the early church in the Acts of the Apostles. They were challenged by the power of the Holy Spirit, as seen in the lives of the first Christians. The Rev. Michael Harper was invited to the church to give two talks on what it meant to be filled with the Holy Spirit.

Michael records what happened after the final talk in his autobiography *None can Guess*:

> There was a memorable hush and stillness over the entire meeting. No one moved a muscle. You could feel the hunger that was arising. I was just itching to

lay my hands on them! But felt the very definite restraint of the Spirit.

We had a time of silent prayer afterwards, which was broken by the vicar, who began slowly and deliberately to confess his own needs and faults. One by one people expressed their needs, and what they wanted. And that was that. I told them afterwards that the Lord had stopped me praying for them, and that he had a programme worked out. They were not to worry, but in his time they would all receive what they were seeking.

John Perry had been brought up a conservative evangelical. His strong emphasis was on personal conversion, the building up of believers in the faith, and of outreach to the community. In 1964 two incidents happened which changed his life. He became conscious of the Holy Spirit.

This renewal was in its early stages in England. John wanted to find out for himself; so he went to a Fountain Trust meeting to hear David du Plessis, the South African Pentecostal minister. David shared his own experience of the Holy Spirit and illustrated from around the world how Christians from various denominations were entering into a new experience which the Pentecostals called 'the baptism'. John was so incensed with what he heard that he left the meeting before David finished. His worst suspicions were confirmed.

But God was working in John's life, and there was a growing sense of dissatisfaction. He took a few days leave from the parish, and with Gay went to Lee Abbey. Here, surrounded by the beauty of the North Devon countryside, they discussed with others the positive side of the renewal. Although he did not fully understand he returned to the parish with a desire to explore the possibilities.

St. Andrew's had become a separate parish, and a new church building was to rise behind the old tin tabernacle, as it was affectionately known. John wanted the new church to be not just a building but a fellowship of individuals created into a corporate body by the Holy Spirit. He realised that if this was to happen he as leader needed a fresh experience of God. On Michael Harper's second visit his prayer was answered.

The meeting finished, and Michael left to drive home. John waited until the others had dispersed, and locked the church. Although a cold winter's evening, he stood in the car-park. The night was still. Above him stretching from the common to the house tops on the opposite hill was a heaven sparkling with stars. He praised the God of creation. He had done this before, but now it was different. The language he was using was unknown to him.

The vicarage telephone was hardly silent during the next few weeks. Mary, the wife of a local estate agent, called to share her experience. She had been out shopping in Watford High Street. Between ticking her list and making purchases she recalled the church meeting and her prayer that God would fill her with his Spirit. The crowd bustled by. Suddenly she began to experience a filling and empowering. Her thoughts turned to praise and adoration. Harry, the managing director of an engineering factory, was carrying a load of compost to the garden. As he stopped to throw it in a heap it seemed to Harry as if Jesus stood before him, immersing him in his love.

John called together a number of people to pray for a member of the church who was ill. Joan was present.

With her husband 'Smokey' she owned an old people's retirement home. Joan had been converted to faith in Christ late in life, and was seeking to know more. As John prayed for the sick member Joan shook from head to toe. She was sure that her bones were making such a noise that everyone in the room would hear. Suddenly, the shaking stopped, and she was filled with peace and joy. For the first time she opened her mouth in public prayer.

During this initial period of renewal John invited Nicky Cruz of *The Cross and the Switchblade* to visit the parish. Nicky came with a team from Teen Challenge on a cold winter's night when the roads were like rivers of glass. When Nicky rose to speak the little tin church was packed to the door.

Nicky spoke in a thick Puerto Rican accent. He recalled his childhood. His parents had earned their living from spiritualism. From an early age he had spent most of his time on the streets, always fighting, often in trouble with the police. There was a force within which wanted to destroy. When he saw a cripple he would kick the crutches away and laugh. He reacted in the same way when he saw blood.

His teenage years had been spent in gang warfare as vice- president of the Mau Maus. He loved street fighting and in gang 'rumblings' had knifed sixteen members of other gangs.

The congregation listened in amazement.

Nicky told of his meeting with David Wilkerson. He first heard David preaching on a street corner in downtown New York. David told how the Holy Spirit could get inside people and make them clean. He said that in spite of what they had done, the Holy Spirit could make them like new babies.

Tears welled up in Nicky's eyes as he related how for the first time he prayed. He told God that he was sorry for the way he was, and asked to be made good like Jesus.

A hush fell over the church—nobody moved. Nicky invited people to commit their lives to Jesus. Slowly men and women moved towards the front. Roy, the headmaster of the local school, was one of many for whom that evening became a starting point in their search for God.

The prayer group increased. Some, who were a little hesitant, attended to find out what was happening. Often they went away puzzled, only to return a few weeks later to testify to a new experience of the love of God.

The Holy Spirit continued to work deeply in the lives of this group. The winter passed and in the early summer of 1965, Edgar Trout again visited the parish. On a Sunday evening after church there was an open invitation to hear him at the vicarage. He spoke on the need of God's people to be servants of each other. He illustrated this from the life of Christ. An open time of prayer followed. This was a God-given time of repentance. People asked for forgiveness. Hidden resentments were confessed to one another. God led many into a deeper stage in their commitment to him, and to each other.

John, with others, saw the need to share this new life in the community. Canon Harry Sutton, then General Secretary of the South American Missionary Society, conducted a mission. His theme for the fortnight was Christ is the answer.

The outreach was to private homes. With expectancy neighbours and friends were invited to the meetings. Harry shared the reason for Christ's coming, and testified to his reality in his own life. At every outreach meeting at least one person committed his life to Christ, and at the

Sunday services many more took the step. A number who were converted to Christ at an evening meeting experienced the fullness of the Spirit the following day.

Home-groups mushroomed around the parish. John appointed leaders for these. Here, in a relaxed atmosphere, new Christians were instructed in the faith, and shared what God was doing in their lives. Some found the coming of new life a painful process.

As the months passed many discovered what God had done for them in Christ and explored in practical terms the meaning of discipleship. Jesus said: 'If any man would come after me, let him deny himself and take up his cross and follow me' (Matt. 16: 24). It became obvious that discipleship included money, that commitment to Christ involved the heart and the pocket, and some were challenged to give a tenth of their income. Unknown to them they were about to experience a financial miracle.

7

Moving Mountains

IN THE FOLLOWING ten years the fellowship at St. Andrew's has been faced, in addition to the regular giving, with financial challenges in excess of one hundred and twenty thousand pounds. The first of these came in 1965 when the congregation outgrew the tin tabernacle. There were long queues out of the church, down the path and into the road. The cost of the proposed new building was forty thousand pounds, of which ten thousand had accumulated over the years. A week of prayer was fixed to precede the launching of the appeal.

The enthusiasm was tremendous, and the money began to flow in. Families and individuals played their part. John fixed a day of thanksgiving. The church stood in faith trusting that the Lord would supply the money by the proposed date, and allow the building to commence. The Sunday prior to the thanksgiving service John received a letter from a member guaranteeing the outstanding amount. Only five months had elapsed since the launching of the appeal.

The new parish church was consecrated by the Bishop of St. Albans in May 1966. The guarantee was never needed. Great was the rejoicing.

1975, with inflation at twenty-four per cent, was hardly the time to launch a venture costing seventy-two thousand pounds, but the call of faith was to go forth. Pentecost was the only recorded instance when the Lord called his church to wait. The need now was for more space at the church, and additional accommodation for the staff. As the church went to prayer everyone was conscious of the magnitude of the task, but equally sure of God. When his people are obedient to him, he releases all that is needed.

Paul, an accountant who had been taught that the two cardinal virtues were caution and prudence, was appointed treasurer for this new endeavour. He knew that it was foolhardy to undertake any project unless there was every likelihood of it being successful. He had learnt over the years to recognise that 'trust and 'faith' were two words which spelt caution with a capital 'C'.

Paul realised that if he was going to be used by the Lord for this venture of faith then he would have to build up his spiritual life and develop a greater sense of faith. The committee talked about money, administration and planning. All his fears were realised! How could a scheme which cost seventy-two thousand pounds be undertaken with any likelihood of success?

On a camping site in the South of France he found the answer. As assistant leader of the young people's group Paul and his wife Janet met Dudley Ward. Dudley and his wife Jill had come from Canada. They had purchased the tiny village of Entrepierres, which nestled in the hills seven miles from Sisteron in Provence.

Entrepierres was to be a Christian retreat centre. Dudley had signed the purchasing contract without the finance believing that God would supply. Time and again he had been led to buy a derelict house, or building materials. Each time he had had insufficient money when he made the commitment; but when the time came to complete the purchase God had supplied. This had been the pattern of his life for ten years. By the end of the summer Paul had come to believe in the God of the impossible.

Many times the leadership at St. Andrew's had to go forward in faith. How the church responded! It still aimed to give half the annual budget to support missions at home and overseas. Gifts, loans, and covenants flowed into the treasurer's postbag.

One Sunday morning the sidesmen were counting the early morning Communion collection when they noticed there an object in the bottom of the bag. They found an exquisite piece of antique jewellery with a note attached, 'For the appeal—a thank offering to the Lord.' Whenever the response slowed more prayer was called for, and from many secret places the Lord released all that was needed.

God's people grew in faith during this time of financial challenge. As they gave to their limit and beyond, it placed them in a position where, with their families, they discovered their dependence on the Lord, and experienced his provision.

George and Margaret wondered how they could give a tenth of their income. They had three teenage sons. Their commitments were multiplying and inflation was swallowing up any increase they received. They believed God was asking them to lay their financial position before him. At the end of the month they knelt together and offered God their pay slip. 'Here it is, Lord, you direct the spending of it,' George prayed. God took over their financial situation and they were able to give a tenth.

I had always hoped that I would return to New Zealand in the Lord's own time. At various intervals I had tentatively suggested it in prayer. Early one autumn morning I was walking the dog across the common when I heard the Lord say distinctly, 'You shall go, and return to this place.'

During the coffee break that morning I was reading the newspaper when an advertisement regarding air fares to New Zealand jumped out at me. 'Go home,' God said.

I pencilled at the side of the advertisement the total cost for the whole family to travel: one thousand, four hundred pounds. I gasped! Never in my life had I owned a quarter of that amount. Perhaps the Lord was just giving *me* the all-clear to go. My parents had promised two hundred pounds, and I had received a gift of two hundred pounds. I booked a return fare with British Airways for myself and continued to pray for the family. At almost zero hour, after worship one Sunday evening, Stanley, a church leader, told me I was to be given a cheque for one thousand pounds. It represented the gifts of a number of people who had prayed, and been prompted by the Holy Spirit.

We found the truth of the promise of Jesus as individuals, as families, and as a church: 'Give, and it will be given to you; good measure, pressed down, shaken together, running over, will be put into your lap. For the measure you give will be the measure you get back' (Luke 6: 38).

All the needs of the church were met. Seventy-two thousand pounds were supplied. This giving was not a few rich people skimming off their excess, but families digging deep in love.

'Where the major problems are to do with growth,' was

The Church of England Newspapers' headline describing St. Andrew's. As the church increased numerically, John decided to share the pastoral oversight which the Bishop had entrusted to him. He called together mature people in the church who were acknowledged leaders. Included in this group were the full-time staff, the church wardens, and the readers. This was known as the 'pastoral group'.

This group explored what it meant to be committed to one another in pastoral leadership. The Holy Spirit did a work of transformation, so that mutual trust became the basis of oneness in Christ. Every Monday evening we met together to share the Scriptures, to break bread, and to pray.

Pastoral problems were no longer solely John's burden. They were opportunities for the pastoral group to serve the body of Christ. Here the understanding of a neurological surgeon was combined with that of an accountant and a factory manager. Here problems were seen in their right perspective and corporate decisions taken.

In Christian leadership the problem of isolation is real. I have suffered from this. Leaders become the focal point of criticism when difficulties arise.

John knew this danger. He allowed the pastoral group meeting to be the place where the leaders could unload the problems of their particular responsibilities. In my ministry of evangelism, although the responsibility is mine, the burden is shared by the group.

Under a corporate leadership the spiritual renewal brought a flowering of faith. There came a time when we reasoned in this way:

Looking back, we can see how the Holy Spirit has

worked among us. In his working there have been many similarities with the activities of the church as recorded in the Acts of the Apostles. On this basis can we expect greater miracles in the future?

8

The Healing Touch

DENNIS CLIMBED THE hill leading to the church. The early summer sun was falling behind the trees which spanned the distant common. The gentle rays streamed through the light green leaves into the valley. The car-park was filling up for Sunday evening Holy Communion at St. Andrew's. Groups were striding expectantly towards the vestibule. This was a service which Dennis always anticipated. As an underwriter at Lloyd's his days were full. At this service he experienced the feeling of belonging to a large caring family. Here he could sit in a peace which eluded him in the rush of the week.

Dennis would have considered himself a seeker rather than a believer. He had heard aspects of the Christian faith which made sense, but he had never let God control his life. This evening was to be different. When his turn came to receive the sacrament he knelt at the communion rail. As he raised his hands the minister placed the bread in them with the familiar words, 'Take and eat this in remembrance that Christ died for you.'

The words exploded in his mind. He thought of the countless millions of people who had lived on earth since creation. Yet Christ had died for him. Had he been the only person on earth, Christ would still have died—just for him.

When the service ended Dennis quietly left. The revelation in the Communion service remained with him. He sang as he ran down the hill and up the other side to his home. A broken relationship which had existed between him and God had been healed.

Alan had knelt at the same communion rail in great pain. The doctors had diagnosed a disease which resulted in a gradual and painful degeneration of the spine. He had spent a long spell in hospital, and although the rest had helped the pain was always with him.

John Perry bent down and asked his request. Alan indicated that he believed that the Lord could heal his back. The clergy and church-wardens prayed with the laying on of hands. Alan felt a warmth seeping down into his spine. He returned to his pew and the pain began to dispel. Within a few days he was completely healed.

Prior to his own renewal John had believed that such healings belonged to the New Testament. He had accepted the theory that such miraculous signs accompanied the coming of Christ, and remained for a time in the early church when it was surrounded by a hostile culture. Today our society was nominally Christian, and medical discoveries had replaced the need for the miraculous.

John, with the church, considered the possibility of Christ healing today. His faith was to be sorely tested.

'I'm afraid,' the specialist said, 'that the leg operation we have in view will not after all be possible . . . Has the surgeon made the alternative clear to you?'

'Yes,' Harold replied, 'the amputation of my leg above the knee.'

Harold had cancer. The specialist had advised an immediate amputation. Harold was a man of exceptional vision who had stood in the place of faith over the money for the new church. He had rallied the faint-hearted to trust in the Lord.

When his bad news was shared with the fellowship many believed that Jesus would heal Harold. He was a key leader. After an evening service the congregation remained for prayer. Expectancy was high as hands were laid on him in the Name of Jesus.

No one doubted that God would intervene. A healing such as this would profoundly affect the community and beyond. This would be a sign that could not be ignored. The congregation dispersed, taking a prayerful concern with them into their homes. Jesus had done so much. Folk had been converted. Believers had been filled with the Holy Spirit. Financial hurdles had been taken, and the Lord had supplied needs from most unlikely places. Optimism was high. A tide of renewal was sweeping the valley.

Harold's condition deteriorated, but faith remained high. There were incidents in Scripture which recorded gradual healing. The man who was blind was a case in point. Jesus had healed him in two stages. Little prayer groups sprang up, and joined with scores of individual households in almost continuous prayer. On the evening before Harold went to hospital for the amputation, thirty people assembled at his home, and shared a simple service of the breaking of bread. The fellowship had experienced before that God's last moment is a long time past man's last moment. Alas, Harold was not to recover. Within a year he was dead. For John, this was a shattering experience.

What on earth was God up to? Were those who had

relegated the miraculous to the first century right after all? There was still an area beyond the frontiers of discovered medicine in which there was no known cure. Here Harold had found himself. Jesus had been present, but in physical terms there was no healing. They had not prayed, 'Father if it be thy will.' They had specifically claimed healing, and it had not been granted.

Some suggested that Harold's death was due to a lack of faith. Had unbelief prevailed? Others now thought that they had possibly been trying to hold God to ransom. If Harold had been healed, all that they were coming to believe about the Holy Spirit would have been authenticated. The fellowship was badly shaken.

John Appleton looked desperately ill as he walked down the aisle supporting himself on two sticks. He had come to church to seek the Lord's healing. The previous week he had asked John if he could have prayer in the church following the evening service. If concern and sympathy could have healed then he would have bounded down the church a whole man.

Medical opinion had forecast a long and painful ending to John's life. The evening following our prayer he went into a deep coma and within three days was dead. In the days between, his wife Jean re-discovered Jesus.

At the end of that year John Perry stood back and asked what they as a church had learnt? Whatever the misunderstandings, the wrong motivations, one fact emerged. There was a new loving concern for the sick and suffering. Besides the after-church prayer meetings, groups had sprung up to intercede. The sick had been sensitively visited.

After his operation and during a time of remission

Harold had written an article for the church magazine entitled 'The Rainbow through the Rain'.

> Perhaps the prayer and sympathy I received sounds quite ordinary and just what one should expect. Perhaps also I should have been able to find comfort and consolation through my own prayer alone. But I am trying to be honest and I must therefore testify that not only was the sense of fellowship far deeper than I should ever have expected, but also that it was in actual fact mainly through this human fellowship that the divine comfort and consolation came to me. I felt as never before a member of a body, a member whose suffering was being shared in a very real way by the other members. For me the New Testament church had come alive and through that church and its loving fellowship I received a new assurance that God is indeed a God of love.

Concern for the individual was expressed by the congregation at the monthly evening Communion Service. Healing was now taken out of the context of the purely physical into an area which embraced the whole man. Those asking for specific prayer were encouraged to communicate last and to stay kneeling whilst the clergy, the wardens, and the readers prayed for them with the laying on of hands.

Trout Stream Hall is a residence for retired missionaries, on the Chorleywood road on the outskirts of our parish. Olive, its warden, suffered increasingly from arthritis. Her joints were swollen, and the pain was no longer checked by drugs. Olive came forward for prayer at the Communion Service. After the service she experienced the most excruciating pain. That night the pain continued to build up in intensity until she felt as if she could bear it no longer. A crisis was reached in the early hours, after which she went to sleep. On awakening the arthritic condition had gone.

Why was she physically healed and not others? It would have been just as easy for God to have touched Harold. These are questions for which we had no adequate answer. The cynic in reaction to Harold's death might say that God doesn't heal the sick. Such a reaction refuses the possibility of a miracle. It ties the hands of God. Others, hearing of Olive, could fall into an equally wrong attitude which results in hopes being falsely raised, so that when terminal sickness or death intervene faith is damaged. Our response lay in neither of these extremes, but in the loving prayer and involvement of the congregation for the individual.

It has been my privilege to pray for others and to be prayed for at this service. I have prayed for many like Dorothy. She hobbled forward on sticks obviously in great pain. Her request was not that God would heal her, but that she would know his peace in an impending operation. We committed the surgeon's hands and skill, and the nurses' patience and gentleness to God. Dorothy was not going alone into a large impersonal ward. We were taking responsibility for her. The Holy Spirit within us was embracing her with his love.

Before going overseas I asked for prayer at this service. As the congregation lifted me to the Lord I sensed a release from fear and anxiety. I was a part of the Body of Christ. In their prayer they were accepting responsibility for my ministry. I could confidently commit my wife and children to them. Travelling thousands of miles from home I was at peace. The healing community embraced me across the seas.

The church was becoming a healing community but we realised that if we lived to ourselves, then we would die by ourselves. The gift of the Holy Spirit to the church was to energise it so that its life could flow out into the world. Failure meant stagnation.

There is a picture which the Holy Spirit gave in relation to our church. It is a picture of a spring of water bubbling up and overflowing in the midst of the people. The water laid around until people commenced to dig trenches which enabled it to flow out into the desert places. The function of leadership is to provide the channels through which this life can flow into the community. The Holy Spirit has the plans for these channels.

9

Captured by a Vision

How could this new life be channelled into the community and beyond? How could we share our faith with people who had no church affiliation? As I was wrestling with this problem, I read the beginning of Mark's Gospel, and noticed a significant truth. From this and the other Gospels, it is evident that Jesus hardly ever tried to communicate alone. When he announced the beginning of his ministry, before anything of significance happened, he called four men to be with him. The five became a team.

What we needed was a team, a group of four or five Christians committed to the Lord and to each other, and to seeking the Holy Spirit's way ahead.

I met Alan at a party. He was the factory manager of a small fibre-glass firm, and in his spare time ran a much sought-after travelling Disco. Alan had been in hospital with a disease of the spine. During this time he came to a faith in Jesus Christ through listening to a Billy Graham broadcast from West Germany. This experience changed his life, and he joined us at St. Andrew's. He was a natural communicator and shared his faith easily. I thought I had found the first member of the team.

John was the exact opposite of Alan. He was a businessman with his own expanding company. He revelled in the thrust of big business, and from the world's point of view had made his mark. John had found a faith in Christ in a Pentecostal chapel.

Janet came from a Christian family, and was a studio manager with the B.B.C. and, with my wife Mary, she completed the five.

We invited the proposed team to our home, and during the course of the evening outlined our vision. After discussion and prayer we decided that we would each ask one other person back to our home on the following Monday evening. There would be a discussion on the meaning of life. I prepared a short introductory starter entitled 'Reflections'.

I have reflected again on the greatness of man,
  I have seen the boundless cities that he has built;
The gigantic buildings seeming to pierce the sky;
  Large areas of water spanned by curving bridges;
Broad motorways sweeping from the cities—packed
  with speeding vehicles.
I have watched jets take off to link continents
  As roads once linked villages . . . I have seen a
    global village.
  In all these things, man is revealed as . . . the
    architect, the designer,
      the engineer . . . .

I have reflected on man's conquests;
  Noticed how diseases have been controlled or
    overcome,
How crops have been blessed by science,
  How famine is being slowly met by birth-control,

How ignorance (so often the cause of death, disease,
squalor) is being met with education.
Here is man—brilliant in intellect—decisive in
action—innately resourceful.
Modern man has come of age.
He realises that his only hope is the increase of his
own power,
For no greater power will help him.
He is optimistic.

I have reflected again on the writings of other
men . . . sensitive men
thinking men . . .
Of Thomas Hardy . . . of Sartre . . . and Camus
Men who, like surgeons, have probed deeply into
the make-up of man.
They write of a world which has no explanation;
Of man who experiences passion without peace;
Who experiences guilt without forgiveness;
Who experiences regret without hope,
Ambition without fulfilment . . . loneliness . . . and
death.
I have reflected on how man has sought to find
freedom from passion . . . guilt . . . regret . . .
ambition . . . loneliness . . . death.
Man has turned to drugs . . . tainted sex . . . craved
for money
Created new experiences . . . grasped for more
knowledge . . .
Is there any solution?

There were more present than we had anticipated. We began with coffee, and after introducing ourselves read

'Reflections'. It was as if nobody had heard. When I asked for comment, one guest raised the question of the Church Commissioners. 'If the church does have a concern for the poor and down-trodden, why doesn't it sell its shares and give the money away?' This became the great issue of the evening and everyone pitched in. By the second coffee break we had left the church's finance, and passed on to the vicar. 'Why do vicars live in such large houses, and support the establishment?' 'When Aunty was dying, why didn't he come when he was notified?' 'If the vicar is a man of God, why did he fall out with my father?' 'Why are those who go to church such hypocrites?'

It was by now the third coffee break; the lounge was so clouded in cigarette smoke that those sitting across the room were hardly visible. I glanced at my watch as someone began to talk about Buddha; it was one a.m. 'All ways lead to God, and man's belief is conditioned by the continent he happens to be born in.' 'Christianity is just a Western religion, and in my opinion rapidly losing ground.' 'In England, humanism has replaced religion and does more for people than Christianity.' 'Man is basically good, with an occasional bad lot like Hitler or Stalin.' The conversation had been in progress for almost six hours. The team had hardly spoken, let alone shared their faith in Jesus. Those we had invited had so many suppressed opinions that they were unable to hear what we had to say.

All those present wanted to come back again the following Monday. Could they bring a friend? Something was happening, but we didn't know what! As nobody had listened I thought it would be a good idea to begin the second evening with 'Reflections' once again. I had hardly finished when the conversation turned to the occult. It was surprising how many had had 'supernatural' experiences of one type or another. We were open to discuss all subjects raised, but we would not allow people to go over old ground. After hours of talking we had the Church Commissioners, the vicar and the hypocrites, other religions, evil, and suffering behind us. At last someone asked us what we thought!

We began with Jesus, but soon realised that we were presuming too much. A number had not really accepted the concept of God. Our Christian claim that the God of Creation had become a man in Jesus Christ became the point of controversy. It was maintained that such a claim was arrogant, and too exclusive. As the evening progressed we noticed one thing which created interest—personal testimony. Alan shared how he had found Christ in hospital, and of the healing of his back through prayer. Janet shared answers to prayer, which she had experienced since trusting Christ. Whenever we shared personally everyone was on tiptoe. Of course rational explanations were quickly found, but it became evident that the Holy Spirit was breaking through.

John Burns had been having golf lessons. He struck up a friendship with 'the professional', and had invited Jimmy and his wife Ann to the meetings. Over the weeks Jimmy had followed the Christian claims, but had reached a stage when he was definitely in opposition. He held the floor for the latter half of one evening, and I thought this was his farewell speech. During the following week Jimmy sold his house and for technical reasons was unable to move into the one he was buying. John invited him and his wife to stay with him.

This became a crisis week for Jimmy. It was not the house transactions that worried him, but Jesus. He couldn't get him out of his thoughts. As he lay in bed his death, his resurrection, and the coming of the Holy Spirit preyed on his mind. Jimmy came to the end of himself. He asked Ann to leave the bedroom as he wanted to pray. Kneeling by his bedside he asked Jesus to forgive him. Suddenly, he sensed a presence in the room which was characterised by love and power. He stretched out his hand as if to touch him. Jimmy had found Christ.

The following Monday evening we all gathered again. I had purposely not asked Jimmy to say anything. I felt that if he did share, it must come from his own desire. We had been talking for about an hour when Jimmy indicated that he wanted to speak. The atmosphere turned electric as he related how he had found Christ during the week. It was obvious that something profound had happened to Jimmy. Nobody tried to rationalise his experience as the group listened in awe.

Martin came with his wife Jenny. I had met them during the summer. Martin was a salesman for an international company, and that year had been one of their top salesmen. The Holy Spirit began to capture Martin at the same time as Jimmy came to faith. Martin's contacts were legionary, and at one stage people began to travel to the meeting from London. Martin and Jimmy with their wives joined the team, and quickly became the front runners. During that autumn and winter over fifty people attended the Monday evenings. I remember the evening when there were five nationalities present.

The Monday meetings finished as suddenly as they had begun. It may have been the commencement of summer, but somehow I didn't think so. It was rather as if a chapter had been completed. The following autumn we began a home group which we called 'The new communicators'.

We hoped that this would be a training base for others who could then begin similar outreach meetings in the parish. With the new people we worked through the objections to belief which the team had encountered, and the ways we had learnt to communicate the Gospel.

We divided into three teams and planned our first outreach meeting. A few outsiders came, but somehow it never gained momentum. The openness and desire to seek the truth which at first we had experienced were no longer there. The new people we invited did not come as readily, and the magnetism which had originally drawn in so many had gone. Our team meetings were discouraging, and I began to wonder what the Lord wanted us to do.

In my thinking I have often likened the Christian's relationship to the Holy Spirit to that of a yachtsman to the wind. Once the yacht is on a course the crew take in the sail slack and adjust the ropes, so that the boat receives all the available power from the wind. If the wind changes direction the sails begin to flap, and it is then time for the helmsman to alter course. He gives the command, and turns the tiller as the boom swings across the cockpit. For the crew there is a moment of uncertainty as they adjust to the new course.

Often the local church has been given a definite course by the Holy Spirit. Unfortunately, in sailing this course it has become so set that when the Holy Spirit calls for a change of direction it is unable to take it, and as a result drifts along without vision or direction. Whenever there is change the individual becomes vulnerable. His security is threatened, because the change will probably involve new people, and new situations. I have known of parishes that have been so afraid of change that they have made the incoming vicar promise to uphold the 'status quo' during his ministry. Such churches become a venerable memorial to a venerable tradition.

Where the church obeys the Holy Spirit's directions Christians may find themselves in a place of insecurity. Here is an opportunity for faith to be tried and strengthened. From the New Testament it seems that the motto of the first Christians was, 'We are committed to continuous change'. We today need the same motto inscribed above the agendas of our church councils and committees. Failure to respond to the Holy Spirit's leading in these days is to write our own death warrant.

The Scripture says that 'without a vision the people perish' (Prov. 29: 18). A vision is not referring to the minute book of the preceding year to find out what the church did. A vision is the unveiling of what is hidden. It is the future plans and purposes of God for a congregation, which at the moment are hidden, but which the Holy Spirit wants to reveal. The Holy Spirit only reveals the next step—which is all the pilgrim church requires.

The end of the Monday evenings, and the subsequent training programme also heralded the time for me to depart to take up my ministry in a second church. For Mary and I the sails were flapping; we were unsettled. I had known since the experience at Athletic Park in Wellington, that my call was that of an evangelist. Unfortunately, the official ordained ministry of the Anglican church consists only of bishops, priests and deacons. One way forward would have been to launch out in faith, believing that the Lord would create the openings and supply the resources, but such a move could lead to isolation and loneliness. The characteristics of all the New Testament ministries were that they were based upon local churches. At Ephesus the apostle, prophet, evangelist, pastor and teacher were part of the leadership of the local church. I began to wonder whether our church would support such a ministry.

During one of the children's half-terms we went to Lymington for a few days. I love walking in the heart of the New Forest, as here I can daydream of the New Zealand bush, and re-live happy times. As I walked I began to mull over in my mind the concept of 'faith-sharing'. Our initial outreach had been through a small 'faith-sharing' team. If this was increased perhaps it could be a vehicle for taking what we were discovering into other parishes and sharing with them. I could not catch what the Lord was saying, but I felt the wind against the sails. We were moving to another course.

The day before returning to Chorleywood I was reading the Psalms when the Lord spoke to me. In my mind I saw a picture. I was standing on a slight hill, and, looking down on my right, was a field of corn, ripe and glistening in the sun. The field stopped at a roadway. Directly in front of me, and out to the left, the harvest field stretched towards the horizon where purple hills formed the boundary. This faded, then I saw the world spinning in space. Initially, it was featureless, but as I watched, the continents began to emerge, and suddenly became fields of glistening grain.

A familiar Scripture came to mind, the words of the Risen Christ prior to Pentecost. 'You will receive power when the Holy Spirit comes on you, and then you will be my witnesses, not only in Jerusalem but throughout Judaea and Samaria, and indeed to the ends of the earth' (Acts 1 : 8). As I thought on these words, the vision began to have meaning. The field bounded by the road was

Jerusalem, our immediate locality: the fields stretching to the horizon were Judaea and Samaria, illustrating our surrounding and distant localities. The world as the harvest field showed the totality of the calling.

Shortly after our return from the New Forest our church council had a day away together, given to prayer and discussion. I shared with them something of what I believed the Lord was saying concerning the 'faith-sharing' teams. How vital it is for individuals to submit their thoughts and ideas to the corporate mind. The phrase 'It has been decided by the Holy Spirit, and by ourselves' (Acts 15: 28) is a scriptural example for us. The revelation to James was submitted and checked by the leadership of the church. Any action taken was corporate, and involved shared responsibility in its fulfilment.

The church council decided they would retain me on the full-time staff, and set me apart, with 'faith-sharing' teams, for the ministry of an evangelist.

10

Getting it Together

I SAT AT MY desk and scribbled down the names of people on the back of a used envelope. These were the folk who would comprise the travelling 'faith-sharing' team. As I reflected upon the names, God began to show me that I had misunderstood his plan. All those whom I had chosen were similar to myself in Christian insight. Suddenly, I realised that we had to represent a strata of church life—in age, marital status, class background, occupation, and in Christian understanding and experience.

I tore up the envelope and took a fresh piece of paper. Another group of names came to my mind. Within a short time I had listed twenty-five people who might form the nucleus. I wrote to each, outlining the concept and asking them to pray. If they felt that God was calling them to this particular ministry, they were to assemble at our home in a month's time. A few asked for more details, but from the majority we heard nothing. On the evening in question the room was full.

There are certain basic principles which are fundamental to such a 'faith-sharing' team. The first is worship. Worship and 'faith-sharing' are complementary. Worship is Godwards and the outworking of that is 'faith-sharing'. It is basic to 'faith-sharing' that God's people know him experimentally in worship.

When King Solomon arranged for the Ark to be taken to the newly completed temple in Jerusalem, the people assembled to praise the Lord (2 Chron. 5:9 ff.). Musicians with cymbals, harps and lyres, were accompanied by one hundred trumpeters. As the people praised the Lord, the priests could no longer fulfil their normal duties because the glory of the Lord filled the Temple.

How much more should the presence of the Lord be experienced in the era of the Holy Spirit? When in the New Testament the Holy Spirit came upon believers, the response was praise and worship. The great hymns of the past, hymns written by the Wesleys, John Newton and Isaac Watts, were inspired by a response to the realisation of the presence and the power of God.

The springtime of the church is characterised by new music. Music which expresses, and words which convey the new life which is being experienced. Many of the words are taken directly from Scripture, and set to music which the Holy Spirit has inspired. The Holy Spirit wants to give the local church music which is a unique expression of their life together. This does not mean abandoning our musical heritage; it means bringing forth from the church's treasury music both old and new.

What we needed were not brilliant musicians, but a musical group who would commit themselves unreservedly to Christ, and to each other. Unless they truly loved each other all their musical expertise would be useless. For the Holy Spirit could not rest in power upon people who were harbouring grudges and resentments. From within the main team I called together this musical group. Initially it was not to sing, but to explore together through prayer and Scripture study the commitment required by Christ. Gradually we shared with each other, and a fellowship emerged. During times of informal worship a new type of music evolved. The Holy Spirit gave words and music to members of the group. This music became an expression of a common life and commitment.

The function of those who lead the worship is not to give a performance or to sing a list of songs, but to be inspired by the Holy Spirit. I first experienced this when I went to Cornwall with a Fisherfolk team led by Mikel Kennedy from the Church of the Redeemer, Houston, U.S.A. I was speaking at the various meetings, and stood with them while they were singing. There was a moment when an invisible conductor took over the group. It was as if a circle had been drawn around us, and the glory of heaven had descended. During such times I was not conscious either of the congregation or of the group. Both had been replaced by a desire to worship the Risen and Glorified Christ. Subsequently, I have travelled with them and had similar experiences in Truro, Norwich and Exeter cathedrals.

David was appointed to lead our musical team. He realised that it was impossible to manuscript the new music, rehearse the teams, and travel at weekends as well as hold down an engineering job. He decided that to have the necessary time to lead this aspect of the ministry he would need to find a job in which he could work a three-day week, and give the remainder of the time to the ministry. His employer, a Christian, was prepared to employ him on this basis.

Under David's leadership our musical group 'Harvest'

saw new forms of worship and music being created.

One of the most crucial features of any church is its relationships. The heartbeat of the Gospel is 'forgiveness'—not just as a theory. Jesus taught fiery Peter that the extent of personal forgiveness was infinite. He himself lived this teaching, praying at the cross for the forgiveness of the Roman soldiers.

Forgiving includes acceptance and a lack of condemnation. It is a foundation upon which all people everywhere can meet. It is the power which turns the other cheek, and welcomes the unlovely. One of the members of the 'faith-sharing' team voiced the thoughts of the majority when she said, 'If I was choosing this team, these would have been the last people I would have chosen.' The challenge became obvious. Unless we could experience a common life and unity of faith, there would be nothing to share.

As in the musical group, now with the whole team we commenced with informal worship. We found that as we praised and worshipped the Lord, he spoke to us through the Scriptures, and the gift of prophecy. Our faith found a unity in diversity as we shared from the Scriptures and our personal experiences of Christ. Relationships were worked out, and we found that we were not individuals to be feared, but to be trusted and loved.

Now we had a 'faith-sharing' team, and a full-time evangelist, all supported and sent out from the local church. Our Diocesan Bishop, Robert Runcie, Bishop of St. Albans, gave us encouragement. But alas, we had nowhere to go. During this waiting time I had a telephone call from a vicar in Doncaster. He had heard about the team, and invited us to visit his parish in two years' time. I felt like saying that we could go the following weekend, but restrained myself, and asked him to put particulars in the post.

The Rev. Michael Harper invited me to accompany him on a tour of the Churches of South India. A number of bishops had issued the invitation. The itinerary took us to Bombay, Hyderabad, Madras, Bangalore, Madurei, returning again to Bombay. Travelling with Michael introduced me to new ways of ministry, which were to be a valuable preparation for the team. On returning I found that we had received many invitations, with the Holy Spirit as the initiator. Within a year we had two teams to meet the growing demand.

Whenever the word evangelism is mentioned it conjures up pictures. For some it is a large stadium full of people being addressed by an American. For others it means conversion, emotionalism, or being asked 'Are you saved?' In the early church, the evangelists were the mouthpiece of the Body of Christ, thrust into areas where faith was met with unbelief. They spoke of Jesus with authority because they had experienced him both individually and corporately within their local church. Surely that should be the pattern for today.

11

On the Road

As the months passed, and we travelled together, certain facts began to emerge. The Holy Spirit was creating 'Arks'—places in villages and in the heart of large cities where Christ was alive, and denomination and churchmanship were irrelevant.

Late one afternoon I was away preparing to speak at a church meeting before a 'faith-sharing' weekend. I sat quietly in the lounge of the vicarage, and thought about the new life we were seeing. I recalled the story of Noah and the Ark.

In the days of Noah the nation was characterised by its violence and lawlessness. People had rejected God. God's reaction was one of mercy and of judgment. He called Noah and commanded him to construct an Ark. To this the call was given. Here protection and provision were to be found as the flood waters rose. Today God was creating new 'Arks'.

St. Luke's, Hackney, is an example. Charles May and his wife Joyce went to the church nine years ago. They inherited a small congregation of evangelical tradition, the product of ten years' hard work by their predecessor. At one stage the bishop had wanted to close it.

A number of years prior to their arrival at Hackney Charles and Joyce had experienced a spiritual renewal. Now they believed that what God had done for them, he could do for others in an East End parish. They were not disappointed.

An Ark is an apt description of St. Luke's. The old Victorian building is dwarfed by high rise flats, which house a cosmopolitan community. Spiritually the area is a desert where the people have no church-going tradition. Yet the congregation reflects a strata of that community. Besides the East-Enders there are families from Africa, Asia, and the Far East. Worship in the church is flexible. The African rhythm and the East-Enders' spontaneity combine in an expression of praise to God.

Charles and Joyce concentrated on building up this family. In the last five years the offerings have increased from nine hundred pounds a year to five thousand. Half of this they give to support missionary work. I spoke with a number of new members. Previously they had not been Christians, but had heard of an 'Ark'. They found God, and joined the family.

As our teams visit such parishes we have the opportunity of sharing our own faith. Mostly we find that the new life is just beginning. Our sharing awakens and encourages faith. I spoke with a church leader after one session. For most of his life he had tried to be good, but was continually frustrated. That morning, during discussion time, he understood for the first time why Christ died. He realised that it was no longer a question of trying, but of living in a personal relationship with God.

In places where the renewal is past its elementary stages there is a desire to explore what this means in corporate terms. In these situations we are able to share what it has meant for us to discover each other, and the gifts which God has given. At the conclusion of a discussion on commitment a young wife ran sobbing from the room. For many months she had been resentful and aggressive towards her vicar. As she considered what it meant to belong to one another this wrong relationship came into sharp focus. She asked her vicar's forgiveness, and a new relationship commenced.

In the 'Arks' there is a healing which is deeper than just the healing of relationships. During my theological training, Dr. Frank Lake, the Director of the Clinical Theology Centre in Nottingham, visited the college, and gave a series of lectures on psychiatry. In a jocular way he suggested that the average Anglican congregation comprised three types of people. The 8 a.m. Holy Communion congregation were the anti-social; the 11 a.m. matins congregation were the depressives; and the 6.30 p.m. evening prayer congregation were the positively matey. Jocularity aside, it would be true to say that many of us who attend our services, and who comprise the Body of Christ, are in need of spiritual and psychological healing. Some are crippled by guilt, anxiety, tension, anger, insecurity, resentments and hurts from the past. In the sacraments of the church they find comfort, but their actual problems remain embedded in mind or spirit.

Iain, our church warden, is a neurological surgeon. His specialised ministry in the 'faith-sharing' team is to speak on the problems of anxiety and tension. When this is held in the afternoon and the seminars are optional his talk usually attracts at least sixty per cent of the conference. Iain shows with illustrations the causes of our spiritual and psychological problems, and relates the healing of these to the person of the Lord Jesus Christ.

Members of the team share from their experience how they are finding healing in the areas which the talk has covered.

This application of the Gospel can be a revelation to those who hear. Jane, for example, took two hours to get out of bed and dress. Her home was her sanctuary, and only immediate family were allowed across the threshold. Each day had its obsessions. There were times when she washed her hair, and hours of the week when she went shopping. She was unable to cope with her young family, and her husband had to take extra responsibility for them.

As Iain showed how our past experiences affect our present behaviour Jane saw new hope. She realised that her adoption had been a major factor in her condition, and that Jesus could bring healing to her. During a time of prayer she asked him to do just that.

A year later I sat in her husband's study.

'I would never have believed that God could change a person so completely unless I had seen it with my own eyes,' he said with gratitude.

'In what way?' I asked.

'Jane has had a personality change. The old Jane has died, and in her body a new person has been created. She gets up in the morning and takes responsibility for the children and the home. We are entertaining. People are calling, and sometimes friends stay. Believe me, it's the greatest miracle I've seen.'

During Iain's seminars Christians see why they act the way they do, but above all they receive hope. As Christians find the answer to their own needs they are able to understand and help those who come seeking answers.

There is an ever-increasing interest in the experience of the Holy Spirit. In one of our teams Stanley and his wife

Joan lead a seminar. Stanley's work as a managing director of a printing firm brought him to Chorleywood. In his previous church he had been very active preaching, helping with administration, leading home-groups, and taking part in evangelistic missions. At St. Andrew's he was challenged by the full church, and the apparent signs of life. With Joan he joined a mid-week series of talks which explained the work of the Spirit.

After one meeting he returned home and in his lounge prayed that the Lord would forgive him and remove any barrier to his receiving the blessing of the Spirit. He asked the Lord to grant him this blessing and confirm it by granting him the gift of a prayer language. He commenced praising God, and as he did so his prayer was answered.

At this seminar many misunderstandings are talked out, and Christians are encouraged to appropriate all the resources of Christ, which they received at conversion. Robert as a young man was brought up in a lively evangelical church. At university and teacher training college he was a leading member of the Christian Union. He married and brought up his family in the same way. His religious discipline involved daily reading of the Scriptures and prayer. Yet he was conscious of a lack of reality and power. Until taking part in the group he had never thought about the gifts of the Spirit. The awareness of these led him to seek and find.

The Holy Spirit's gift of prophecy has been a source of inspiration and encouragement to the teams. It has also been a means, as the Apostle Paul indicated, of bringing men to Christ. On a Saturday evening during prayer a team member spoke a word of prophecy. Its message was that God is love and that where love is, fear has no place.

After the family service the following morning a man returned to the church who had been with us the previous evening and had heard the prophecy. He had been a church attender for a number of years, but had been afraid of committing his life to Jesus Christ. Through the word of prophecy God had spoken to him. At the conclusion of the morning worship he commenced to drive his family home. They had travelled half-way when he was compelled to return to the church, where we were able to pray with him.

We are part of a renewal where Christians are wanting to apply their faith to family, business, and recreation. It is not only the 'faith-sharing' teams which share their insights in these seminars. Everybody has a contribution to make. Insights which for years have been hidden are drawn out, and faith is generated. It is as difficulties are voiced that Christians warm towards each other, experiencing an unfreezing.

Spring is a celebration of life. When the prodigal son returned the father's words were, 'Bring the calf we have been fattening, and kill it. We are going to have a feast, a celebration, because this son of mine was dead and has come back to life; he was lost and is found. And they began to celebrate' (Luke 15: 23–24).

When the teams are travelling, Saturday night is celebration night. This is an opportunity to bring together all that the Holy Spirit has been teaching. Folk give testimony to new understanding and experience into which they are entering. 'Harvest' leads us in fun songs and praise, and the team perform one of Janet's plays. It is an expression of our life together.

The climax of the weekend is the Sunday evening Holy Communion. An invitation is given for those who would like specific prayer to make their Communion last of all, and to stay kneeling at the altar rail. On behalf of the praying church, the leaders pray with the laying on of hands.

I was travelling in the west country in June. The day had begun fine and sunny, but about midday there was a deluge of rain. The shower lasted no more than five minutes, but its intensity was so great that streams of water flowed down the highway. After the storm had cleared the sun continued to shine. That is how it is when God pours out his Spirit I reflected.

The seeds in the fields need rain to germinate and grow. Without the rain there is no growth. As the church prays the Holy Spirit falls like rain upon the seeds of faith. After such an outpouring of the Holy Spirit we see the growth.

In every sphere of faith-sharing, the Holy Spirit must provide the initiative. He is the one who wants to reveal Christ, and bring men into a relationship with him. The team was invited to one parish where the vicar shortly after his arrival had experienced a spiritual renewal. He had invited us with trepidation because he had no idea who, if any, would involve themselves in the conference. After a few of our team had met the church council I was reassured.

When we arrived the Holy Spirit had so drawn the people together, that our presence seemed superfluous. The conference was well attended, and on the Sunday the church was packed, with members of the congregation standing in the gallery. I preached a Gospel message interspersed with testimonies by team members. At the conclusion of the service many received Christ. One man, in his middle forties, had last been to church as a teenager.

During the previous two months he had experienced a desire to seek God. Now he found him.

During this weekend those who comprised the 'Ark' in that church captured a vision of what they could be. Subsequently, there was a desire to meet together and share with one another. A concern developed for those in the community who did not know Christ. As a result, John, their vicar, invited neighbours and friends into their home to hear about Jesus. There was a great awakening, which involved sixty-five homes and over six hundred people.

Our parish sent a team of one hundred to share in groups of four. Each unit had a leader who was responsible for guiding the evening. After coffee, and a time when each team introduced themselves, the leader spoke on Christ for today. Other team members gave a testimony and discussion followed. For the agnostic, with no church background, this was an opportunity to consider in a relaxed atmosphere the claims of Jesus Christ. For those who were seeking to know God it was a discovery of the way.

At the end of one house-meeting I felt that the Holy Spirit had led a couple to where they might make a commitment. I wanted to speak to them alone, but there was no opportunity. We had barely reached our car when I was called back. They both wanted prayer to receive Christ.

At another mission a lady in our group had recently lost her husband. They had been holidaying together on the Continent when he collapsed and died. In the discussion she commenced by saying how resentful she felt towards God, and then recounted her experience. As the team sensitively talked of the risen Christ her attitude changed. She wrote in her parish magazine:

The most wonderful experience of my life happened to me during the Alive '75 week. It is most difficult for me to describe it in words, but I will do my best.

I was invited to a house meeting to meet some members of the team. Most of the other people there were strangers to me too. We began the meeting by each person introducing himself or herself and giving a little about the background of their lives. John and Clare, who led the meeting, told us of their own experiences and of Clare's difficulties at one stage in her life.

Suddenly it was as though the flood gates opened within me, and out came the pouring of my bitterness against God and life because of the loss of my dear husband so unexpectedly and tragically whilst on holiday abroad this summer. It sounds trite to say I received comfort from that group of people. What I did receive was love. An overwhelming feeling of something so powerful. For the first time in months I did not cry myself to sleep and was able to really pray.

It is springtime in the church.

THE END

BILL BAIR

Love is an Open Door

'I want you to quit your job and start working with the kids I will bring to you.'

These are the words Bill Bair thought he heard at a church service. Bill had progressed in 18 years from a ditch-digger to an executive position with the gas company. Could God really be asking him to do this?

The young people who come to Bill's door are problem kids – drop-outs, drug addicts, school failures.

'A poignant, memorable story . . . a heartwarming book.' – *Methodist Recorder*

'Very readable . . . so full of warmth and love. I couldn't put it down.' – *Buzz Magazine*

'One man's and his family's response to Christian experience and human need . . . commanding reading.' – *Church of Ireland Gazette*

COLIN URQUHART

When the Spirit Comes

'Something different was needed; not just praying for sick people, but healing them!'

When the Reverend Colin Urquhart began his ministry as parish priest of St Hugh's, near Luton, on a large housing estate, he knew from the experience of his predecessors that life would be tough.

Within four years, however, his church had changed beyond recognition as the members found themselves witnessing miracles of healing, and establishing new relationships with one another as God gave them a remarkable vision of love, community and service.

'A gem ... people praising God ... all happening on an English council estate!' – *Buzz Magazine*